Chapter 1

It was just after lunch when the phone rang at the Siyagruva Dance Studio. Thabiso Khoza, who managed the studio, needed a quiet afternoon to sort through the month's accounts, so he was annoyed at the interruption.

'Siyagruva, how can I help?' he snapped as he answered the phone. Ten minutes later, he was doing all he could not to scream *'Thank you ... Thank you ... I love you!'* at the caller on the other end of the line.

'Yes, of course,' he said instead, as calmly as he could. 'Yes, no problem. See you all on the 25th, and thank you for this opportunity.'

He put the phone down carefully, pinched himself to make sure he wasn't dreaming, and then screamed out loud, *'Yesss!!!!!!!!'*

In the studio next door, the dance instructor, Raymondo, stopped counting the beats to which the Siyagruva dance group had been working out. The dancers all stopped mid-step. Thabiso's scream was that loud!

'What's going on?' Raymondo asked impatiently. He didn't have to wait long for an answer. Thabiso burst through the swing-doors, his wheelchair spinning him to the centre of the room, a broad grin on his face.

What had happened? Thabiso was usually very cool and professional while practice sessions were going on.

'Okay, take five, everyone,' Raymondo ordered, and the dancers relaxed. They surrounded Thabiso in his wheelchair.

'Can you believe it? She – "the original Venus" – is coming here! Here! In two weeks' time!'

'What are you going on about?' asked Sam impatiently. She was upset because she liked to think that *she* was the original Venus.

Thabiso smiled patiently at Sam. '*Ndiyaxolisa* – sorry, baby sister, I didn't mean to diss my queens, but this woman ...'

'Who?!' everybody demanded at the same time.

Thabiso took a deep breath.

'Nandi Xaba.'

He waited for the information to sink in.

Raymondo sat down suddenly.

'I don't believe it!' was all he said.

Zadie, Sam and Shelley (whose nickname was Percy, which she hated) turned away. For a minute they had hoped he was going to say Destiny's Child or someone important like that. But Nandi Whatever – who was that and why should they care?

But Brunette whooped with joy and danced around like a mad thing.

'I can't believe it, I can't believe it,' she sang.

Thabiso clapped. 'Oh, thank goodness somebody knows something, otherwise it would be too much! *Batjele*, tell them – *Bafundise iculture* – teach them some culture, Bru.'

Brunette had to get her breath back first.

'Nandi Xaba is only the phattest, coolest contemp dancer in South Africa ... she's from Gauteng, but originally from the Eastern Cape. She's known all over the world, and she features in magazines, even fancy ones like *Elle* and *Cosmo*. Sam and Percy – I'm surprised you didn't see the article about her last month. I thought that mag was your bible.'

'Was she modelling something?' asked Sam with mild interest, because she only ever flipped though the fashion pages and, sometimes, if she was really bored, she read her star sign, but nothing else.

Brunette shook her head. 'Anyway, she's

really cool. She does all kinds of good stuff too.'

'Oh,' said Shelley, taking a sudden interest. 'Does she work with street kids and drug addicts – that kind of stuff?'

'Oh yes,' said Thabiso, earnestly. 'She's beautiful and talented, and her heart's in the right place too! She is the most perfect woman ever!'

'Guess who's in lurve!' sang Disi. His real name was Mncedisi but he'd got really tired of saying it over and over to people who didn't speak isiXhosa and who couldn't or wouldn't pronounce it properly, so he put up with 'Disi'.

Rashaad, on the other hand, didn't mind being called Rash – that was his official nick-name. He had already been 'To-Die-For' (TDF) when he first joined the dance group, but now that he was body-conscious and more confident, he was really breaking hearts without even knowing it. Behind the closed doors of the girls' toilet, they said he was seriously dishy. He had the 'S-factor'. That was the code the girls used when they wanted to talk about him or any other dishy guys in the area.

At that moment, Rash should have been packing up, leaving the Siyagruva studio, and making his way to mosque. He wasn't supposed to miss Friday evening prayers. He had promised his parents – it was part of the deal to let him come to the dance sessions on Fridays. But now he was in a playful mood, so he swept Shelley up off the floor and they ended their little dance in a romantic dip. Rash bowed to Shelley, then spun away, leapt into the air and collapsed on the floor, clutching at his heart, moaning, 'Oh, Nandi X!', while Shelley blushed almost purple.

Thabiso was in too much of a good mood to be teased about his crush.

'Listen up!' he said more seriously. 'We've been chosen to co-ordinate some workshops that Nandi X wants to run while she's in town. So, I'll draw up lists. It will be quite easy to reach our own communities, but we'll have to choose carefully because she can only do three different venues. Anyway, let's find out which venues are available – that's your homework for this weekend. Oh, yes! And in return, we've got front-row seats at her performance. And ... we're invited to the party afterwards to meet her! That's all for now. I've got so much to plan. This visit must go off perfectly!' He spun his wheelchair around and left as quickly as he had come.

'Well,' said Zadie, 'I don't think the kids in our community will be interested in getting lessons from Nandi X. Nobody knows who she is. What must I say, *mos*?'

Brunette shook her head. 'Try to be a little more positive – they don't have to know everything about her. When I saw Nandi X, I was just twelve. We used to go to the Market Theatre in Jozi to see plays because of my mum being an actress and all, but this was the first time I had ever seen a dance performance. It really inspired me. She was amazing! So, maybe it's some kid's dream to be a dancer, but they just need to know that it's possible. Just seeing Nandi X and knowing that it's possible to become a professional dancer could be the thing that keeps them going through the hard times, that's all.'

She swept out of the studio, feeling very important. But she was also worried. Nandi X! She saw herself at the Artscape Theatre in front-row seats. It would be the first time she had ever gone to such a fancy place.

What was she going to wear? She was still puzzling about this when Shelley came running up behind her and grabbed her by the shoulders.

'Hey, Bru!'

Brunette nearly jumped out of her skin.

'What!?'

'Well, if you're going to be like that ...'

Shelley backed off, looking hurt.

'Ah, come on,' sighed Brunette. 'I was just thinking about what to wear for this fancy "do" we're all invited to. You gave me a *skrik*. Relax, man.'

Shelley smiled and fell into step next to Brunette.

'I need to talk to you,' she said urgently, half-whispering.

They walked together towards the Main Road.

'Well?' asked Brunette after some moments of silence. 'You'd better talk fast because a taxi will be along any minute.'

'Can't I come with you?' begged Shelley. 'It's a long story.'

'How are you going to get back to Gardens?'

'I'll take a taxi ... or I can sleep at your place!'

'Can't you just tell me now, really quickly, then we can talk about it tomorrow?'

Across the street, Shelley's mother climbed out of her BMW. She had been waiting patiently for Shelley to cross the road, but Shelley had been too anxious to talk to Brunette to notice.

'Shelley!' her mom called to her. 'Come on, I've been here for ages!'

A taxi came along the Main Road with its characteristic toot-toot to attract customers. Brunette wanted to miss rush hour, so she got in quickly.

'Sorry, Percy, out of time, let's talk tomorrow!'

The door slammed shut and she was off. Shelley crossed the road and kissed her mother. She wished they wouldn't call her Percy. It was such an old, stale joke, on a dead poet's name – Percy Bysshe Shelley. Anyway, she could hardly wait to see Brunette the next day to get her problem off her chest. If anyone could help, it would be Bru.

Chapter 2

Brunette got to Langa about forty-five minutes later. As she walked home, she thought about what she was going to cook for her father that evening. She had moved from Jo'burg to Cape Town after her parents decided that she needed to spend more time with her dad. He worked for a TV production company in the City Bowl, but he preferred to live in Langa because, he said, life was more sociable there. Brunette was getting used to it. She didn't speak Xhosa so well, but she spoke Zulu, and so tried to remember to say '*Ndi-*' for 'I' instead of '*Ngi-*', and made her Zulu accent more sing-song, the way she thought the language sounded down in Cape Town. And there were some words that were different – for instance, '*thetha*' meant to talk, but in Zulu the right word was '*khuluma*'.

When she got to the front gate, she stopped. She saw 'Auntie' Grace in the kitchen window. Grace was her father's new girlfriend. The two had met while working on a film set, where Grace did some catering. She was a professional caterer. Although she and Brunette's dad had been seeing each other for a month, she had never invaded their kitchen before. Through the window, Brunette could see she was moving between the kitchen sink and the stove. It looked as if she was cooking.

Brunette went in through the front door, and followed the smell of a delicious stew into the hot kitchen. A large pot was bubbling on the nearest burner on the stove. Grace was scraping carrots, wearing Brunette's apron. She looked very much at home.

'*Molo*, Auntie Grace,' Brunette said.

Grace turned from the sink with a big smile on her wide face. She was wearing red lipstick, and it looked too bright against her yellow skin, which was flushed from the heat.

One of these days, she's got to let me give her a makeover, thought Brunette.

'*Awu, molo, sana*!' Grace said, excitedly. 'I didn't see you come in.'

'*Ukhona utata* – is Dad around?'

'He's just popped out to Bra Biza's place. He'll be back at about seven. He said he couldn't miss my home cooking!'

Grace giggled like a young girl. Brunette forced a smile. She cooked for her dad every day! Well, it looked as if she wouldn't be needed tonight, but she offered to help.

'Oh no,' said Grace, waving her away. 'You go and do your homework. I'll call you when it's ready.'

So Brunette went to her room, wondering what to do with this unexpected free time. She didn't have any homework. She started to look through her clothes and tried on a few things. Nothing seemed to fit properly.

'Mmm ...' she thought, 'my clothes are shrinking! What am I going to wear to Nandi X's big night?'

On the other side of town, in Gardens, Shelley was thinking the same thing. She wanted to dress to impress, so shopping was the answer. Yes! What fun it would be to go shopping with all the girls. That way, they could also be sure that none of them turned up wearing the same dress! She had enough time before dinner to call Sam.

'Speak.' That was the way Sam always answered the phone.

'Hi,' replied Shelley.

'Whassup?' asked Sam.

'What are you wearing to the Nandi X thing?'

'To what?'

'Oh, come on, Sam, have you forgotten already?'

'Nah – what are you wearing?'

'I've got nothing. I gave all my old clothes to the homeless!'

'Even that divine "Stoned Cherrie" thing?'

'Even that.'

'You're too much.'

'So we have to go shopping.'

'I'm in.'

So Sam called Brunette. Brunette heard the phone ring. Auntie Grace answered it, talking loudly.

'Oh, she's just doing her homework while I cook us a good meal. Who's calling, please?' Then she called, 'Brunette, *sana*! Sam on the phone for you!'

'Who was that?' asked Sam when Brunette

came to the phone.

'Auntie Grace, my dad's ... er ... friend.'

'Scary!'

'Mmm. She's trying very hard. So?'

'Nobody's got anything to wear, so we're going on an expedition.'

'Oh ... okay.'

Back in her room, Brunette took out her bankbook to see how much she had. She groaned. She had sent most of her money to her younger sister in Jo'burg, to pay for a school trip. With all the dancing practice they had been doing, she hadn't been able to make extra money in the last month. Usually, there was someone who wanted their hair done, or she would do the make-up for a wedding, and the customers would pay her well and tell their friends about her. But last month she had turned down these jobs.

She thought about her dad. She was still shy about asking him for money, and she knew he would suggest that she take on a few jobs. But how, at such short notice? Plaiting hair was an option, but it took so long to do. But ... there was Auntie Grace ... maybe she could give her a facial, and a manicure and pedicure, something quick and easy.

Brunette went back to the kitchen as Grace was putting the finishing touches to the evening meal.

'Auntie Grace,' Brunette said as casually as she could.

'Yes, my darling?'

'I need to make some extra money. We've got this ... thing. I need a new dress. Do you know anyone who needs ... a makeover?'

Auntie Grace mopped her brow with the apron. 'Let me think ... oh yes!'

Brunette waited for her to suggest herself, but instead Grace took her cellphone out of her bag and started going through the numbers. Then she tapped the speed dial.

'*Sis*' Dolly?'

Brunette sat at the kitchen table and listened. Within minutes, Grace had organised for Brunette to plait extensions for Dolly. It was hard work, but her friend Dolly was prepared to pay R200!

'Oh thanks, Auntie! Thank you!'

Auntie Grace beamed. 'No problem. You know I always do my best, don't you?' She paused as if waiting for Brunette to agree, but she said nothing, so Grace quickly went on. 'She's waiting for you now, just so you can see what you need to do. She's three doors away. Hurry now, before supper, but don't be late!'

So Brunette went over to Dolly's house. What luck! she thought to herself, smiling happily on the way there. When she got to the house, she knocked and Dolly came to the door. Brunette almost groaned aloud. Dolly had really short hair and her head was rather large. It would take ages to do!

Dolly knew exactly what she wanted. She wanted tiny little braids using human-hair extensions – which was the worst, because they never did what you wanted them to. On the floor of the lounge, Dolly had laid out magazines. She pointed to pictures of Tyra Banks, the supermodel.

'*Uyabona sisi* – you see, my girl – *ndifuna kubamuhle nje ngaye* – I want to be as beautiful as she is. So, when can you start?'

Brunette sighed. Things were never as easy as you hoped. 'Tomorrow,' she said.

'And when can you finish?'

Brunette touched Dolly's hair and gripped some to see what the texture was like. It slid out of her hand very easily. She would never finish in one day.

'As soon as I can – maybe by Sunday?'

'Okay then, see you tomorrow.'

Back at home, Brunette found her dad was back from Bra Biza's place. Instead of the quiet man who usually sat in front of the television for most of the night, she found him laughing loudly and talking non-stop with Auntie Grace. As she sat down to eat with them, it seemed as if they really wanted to be alone, so she rushed through her supper, washed her plate, and tried to sneak off to her room. She was at the door when her dad said, 'Hey, Brunette *sisi*, where are you off to?'

'I need to fix some things for school, *baba*,' she answered.

'Aren't you going to thank Auntie for the lovely meal, mmm?'

Auntie Grace laughed shyly. Brunette forced a smile.

'Thank you, Auntie,' she said quickly and dashed off.

As soon as she was out of the room, there was a brief silence – they must have been kissing! – and then they both laughed like happy children. Brunette sighed and shook her head. It looked as if her dad was getting quite serious about Auntie Grace. What would happen next?

In her bedroom, Brunette slid the drawer open and took out a bar of chocolate. She chewed quickly as she thought about the different scenarios. What if Auntie Grace moved in? What if they wanted to get married? Then they'd have a baby and she would have to look after it! Would her mum let her move back to Gauteng? Before she knew it, she had finished the whole bar of chocolate.

Chapter 3

The next day was Saturday, and the Siyagruva dance group were supposed to practise for a good part of the day. But because of the arrangements for Nandi X's visit, Thabiso and Raymondo decided that they would practise only in the morning. In the afternoon, they would sort out the arrangements for the tours in the different communities.

As soon as Brunette arrived, Shelley jumped on her again, giving her a dig in the ribs.

'Percy!' Brunette snapped. 'Don't do that.'

'Ooh, touchy, hey ... that time of the month?'

'How original.'

'*Sjoe*, you really are in a bad mood. What's up?'

'Nothing, it's just that you always jump on me and it's really getting on my nerves!'

Brunette regretted her words as soon as they were out of her mouth. Shelley blushed and bit her lip.

'Oh, come on,' Brunette said apologetically. 'I didn't mean it like that. Now, what's the matter with you?'

Shelley perked up straight away.

'I really need someone to talk to.'

'Well, here I am.'

Shelley took a deep breath. 'I ...' She stopped. 'I feel so stupid!'

'What?'

'Okay, here goes ... I think I'm in love.' She grinned.

Brunette nodded her head slowly.

'I don't see a problem so far ...'

'Well, you don't know who I'm in love with.'

'No, you haven't told me.'

'It's ...'

'Come on!'

'It's Rash,' Shelley said, looking closely at Brunette for a reaction. Brunette squirmed.

'Well, you do know that Rash is ...'

'Gay. I know that's what he says, but how did he decide that?'

'It's just the way he feels. He's still trying to figure it out himself.'

'Well, maybe he'll change his mind,' Shelley said hopefully.

'I really don't know, Percy, but I'd say forget it.'

'How can you be so cruel!'

'Sorry, babe, I don't know what to say, unless you speak to him yourself.'

'No!' Shelley grabbed Brunette's arm. 'And don't you dare say anything.'

'So, how's this love supposed to happen or not happen, whatever, if it's a secret?'

'I don't know – and you'd better not tell him!'

'Okay, okay. Relax!'

'Promise?'

Brunette nodded her head. 'Promise.'

Sam came sauntering up to them.

'What are you two talking about, mmm?'

There was an awkward silence. Sam looked from one to the other, her eyes narrowing suspiciously.

'Shopping!' Brunette said brightly.

'Oh yes!' said Sam. 'We have to talk about that.'

Shelley sighed with relief and smiled gratefully at Brunette.

'What are you thinking about wearing, Bru?' asked Sam.

'Not sure yet,' Brunette said quickly.

'Well, I saw the most divine little number at the Young Designers' Emporium ... mind you, there was only a size 32, I think, so it might be a bit small for you.' She prodded at Brunette's waist, frowning. 'Still, you've got a week. Give up the chocolate, girl. It's not doing you any favours.'

Brunette forced a smile.

The girls decided to go shopping the next Saturday because there would be no time before then. Brunette was relieved. At least she'd have a chance to make some money by then.

During practice, Shelley went a bit far trying to get Rashaad's attention. It was embarrassing for Brunette to watch Shelley bat her eyelids at Rashaad and literally throw herself at him while they danced. Poor Rash looked seriously confused and was trying to catch Brunette's eye to signal 'Help!'

Brunette felt really sorry for both of them, but there was nothing she could do except hope that things would work out without anyone getting hurt.

After dance practice, Brunette went to Thabiso's office to let him know that she might not be able to make it for a meeting on Monday evening. She found Thabiso looking at a photo of Nandi X. In the photo, her smile lit up her beautiful face. She was posing, holding a child in mid-air, and you could see the child's wheelchair in the background.

'She's amazing, isn't she?' Thabiso said, looking up at Brunette. 'If I could find a girl like this ...' he smiled a little sadly, and then he snapped out of his mood. 'So, what's up, Bru?'

'Oh ... nothing.'

Brunette left Thabiso looking at the photo. Ah, love! She'd had enough for one day. Everyone seemed to be in love with some impossible dream.

These love things were complicated. One person always seemed to want something more. Then she thought of her dad and Grace, laughing and kissing secretly like teenagers. Maybe sometimes it happens that two people want to be together at the same time, which is fine, except when one of those people has a daughter who is secretly hoping that it won't work out ...

When Brunette got home, she found her dad sitting in the lounge, reading the Saturday newspaper. At least he was alone.

'No soccer today, dad?'

'No, I'm just relaxing. I'll go out later.'

Brunette told him about organising Nandi X's visit to Langa. He was very excited and said he'd speak to some of his colleagues at the TV production company about covering the event. He suggested that she talk to Mama Lillian, who took bookings for the local hall. It was a good suggestion. It meant that she wouldn't have to run around too much. She changed into comfortable clothes, then went round to Dolly's place. Dolly was waiting impatiently.

'I thought you'd come earlier,' she said.

Brunette started plaiting Dolly's hair. Dolly watched a taped Oprah show on TV while Brunette worked, but she still talked nineteen to the dozen. Brunette wasn't really listening, but she said 'mmm ...' and 'ah ...' every now and then. Her attention was focused on Oprah's 'lifestyle makeover' tips. By the end of the show, she was inspired. She had all she needed to change her life. She was going to stop eating chocolate and make the most of Nandi X's visit to promote her skills as a budding beautician.

It was around ten when she got back home, and her feet were aching from standing all day. The house was dark and cold. She had only managed to do about one quarter of Dolly's hair, but her plaits were neat and Dolly was pleased with the progress so far.

Even though she'd had something to eat at Dolly's, she felt quite hungry. One bar of chocolate would be enough to relax her and fill her up. She would start on her new lifestyle makeover plan in the morning.

Chapter 4

The week passed quickly and Saturday arrived. With a huge effort, Brunette had finished Dolly's hair before the week-end, but she was exhausted, and, to keep her energy levels up, she had been munching on chocolate. The day of the shopping expedition was here and she was sure she wouldn't fit into a size 32 dress. But, at least she had money, and could afford a new dress, if she found one she liked.

It was a sunny winter's morning and it didn't look as if it was going to rain that day. She took a taxi into town and met the other girls at the Waterfront. Zadie didn't join them, so it was just Sam, Shelley and Brunette.

'So, where to first?' Brunette asked.

'Oh, *skat*!' sighed Sam. 'Must I teach you everything? We must be civilised and have a cappuccino coffee first.'

'Oh, puh-leeze,' said Shelley, rolling her eyes. 'You're such a poser!'

'And why not?' Sam pouted. 'If you've got it, flaunt it, baby!' And she swished in front of them and waltzed into the first boutique. Brunette looked around. It was the first time she had ever gone inside a place like this.

As she walked, her clumpy boots squeaked on the Italian-tiled floor. A model-like woman came up to them, smiling.

'Hi, Sam!' she said warmly.

'Hey, Mandy!' Sam replied, not too warmly because she was being cool. 'What have you got that's new?'

So Mandy took them to a selection of expensive-looking eveningwear that had just arrived. Brunette wandered off and looked at some other dresses. She lifted one of the price tags and nearly fainted. She didn't have enough money to buy even one sleeve!

On the 'first round', as Sam called it, they just looked and tried on different clothes, without buying anything. They tried different perfumes until they nearly fainted from the mixed fumes.

'I can't breathe!' gasped Brunette, as Sam tried yet another strong-smelling scent. They dragged themselves outside and gulped in the fresh, salty sea air, before going back for 'the second round'. Now it was time for serious shopping.

As Shelley and Sam went back through the shops, Brunette was stunned. It was amazing how they could remember which dress or pair of shoes they had seen in which shop. Brunette told them so.

'If only I could remember my school lessons as well,' admitted Sam. 'I'd be a real whizz-kid, hey?'

Sam bought a knee-length, golden, beaded dress. It looked amazing against her dark skin and it fitted her slender frame snugly. But she also had to get sandals to match, and a bag, and expensive gold make-up made for black skin – all on her mom's credit card. Shelley went with her favourite colour, in a floor-length, burnt-orange dress, with a swooping back and a thigh-high slit.

'What d'you think, Bru? Will it do the job?' she asked, winking as she flashed a long leg through the side slit. She ruffled her blond mop and posed.

'Perfect ... for you,' agreed Brunette.

'Percy, love,' remarked Sam, as casually as she could, 'your fake tan is all streaky.'

Shelley bent over and examined her leg closely. 'Oh, what a pain! I hate winter.'

So, Shelley got some matching make-up, fake tan cream and hair mascara, too.

The cost of all the items made Brunette feel quite ill. She didn't buy anything. She was too embarrassed to count through her measly R300 budget. So she decided to come back alone during the week, and look for something she could afford, as unlikely as that seemed.

By the end of the day, Brunette was thoroughly depressed. She got home to find nobody in. Her dad would probably be spending the night at Grace's. She went to her room, where she sat doing her nails, all the while thinking about where she would find something to wear that looked nice but didn't cost too much. She thought about chocolate but decided to go outside for a smoke instead.

Ah, progress, she thought, smiling to herself. Sam would approve, the cow. She was always going on about how fat everyone was and how fat she herself was, even though she was as skinny as you could get.

Face it, girl, thought Brunette, you're never going be that thin, even if you don't ever eat again. But I can stop eating chocolate, just for myself – not because Sam the cow says I should. I'll save money if I stop eating chocs – at least R10 a week! She looked at her glowing cigarette and thought, and if I stopped smoking a cigarette every time Sam freaked me out, I could save at least R15 a month ... but one thing at a time, I think.

By the end of the evening, she was feeling a lot better. She'd manage. After all, it was more important to be herself than to get all worked up about looking good for one day.

At home, Shelley prepared her tan carefully. Then she tried on her outfit in full. Her mother's dressing room had mirrors all around, so she went in and looked at herself from all sides.

I look amazing, she decided. And if Rash doesn't notice me now, then I really don't know. She took some photos out of her drawer and sorted through the pile, until she got to one of Rash.

'Just you wait, boy,' she said to his photo, 'you won't know what's hit you!'

Although Brunette had managed to cheer herself up, she still hadn't found anything to wear. Also, Auntie Grace was cooking delicious meals almost every night, and then, for dessert, serving up chocolate cake that you couldn't resist. Brunette's dad was working late that week, so it was just the two of them sitting at the table, staring at each other. Brunette ate non-stop so she didn't have to make small talk. Auntie

Grace seemed determined to make Brunette like her.

As she was served up chocolate cake for the third night in a row, Brunette protested.

'Auntie Grace!' she cried. 'I'm supposed to be watching my weight.'

Auntie Grace clucked disapprovingly. 'A growing girl like you – there'll be plenty of time for that later in life. Right now you just need to eat and grow.'

'Grow sideways,' muttered Brunette.

'Anyway, I don't see why you worry. You're not overweight – you look lovely.'

Brunette sighed. There was no point in arguing.

'I ... it's just that all my clothes are tight and I don't have a thing to wear for this big do on Saturday.'

Auntie Grace smiled and clapped her hands.

'Why didn't you say! I'll call Meikie. She's the wardrobe lady for the TV series I'll be working on next month. She makes everyone look like a star and she's got a great little shop.' Auntie Grace smiled. 'Our first shopping trip ... together.'

Brunette turned away and rolled her eyes. What with Grace's over-bright red lipstick and her friend Dolly who wanted to look like Tyra Banks, what on earth would Meikie's 'great little shop' be like?

The dress in the shop window called to her. *'Come and get me!'* it said. So Brunette rushed ahead of Auntie Grace and went into Meikie's little shop, which she had never noticed before, off Greenmarket Square. She was holding her breath, hoping that the dress would be in her price range. It was less than R200 and, even better, it fitted her perfectly. The deep red colour was exactly her shade!

Amazing, thought Brunette, as she spun round and round in the tiny, badly-lit fitting room, there is a God. And then she thought, thank God for Auntie Grace. Maybe I should try harder to like her.

She would have loved to get new shoes to go with it but she had to settle for a dark, almost black lipstick and nail polish. Then she got some burgundy extensions to add to her dreadlocks. Things were definitely looking up. She couldn't afford new shoes but her high-heeled, knee-length boots would do nicely.

It was Friday – the day before the big night. At Siyagruva, Thabiso was in a frenzy, ordering everyone about. They were all involved in cleaning up the studio because Nandi X would be visiting it the day after her performance. Then she'd be holding workshops in Langa, in Lavender Hill and at Westerford High School. Brunette's dad had suggested to his production company that they videotape her visit, and they were excited too. They'd be doing an interview with her and with Thabiso at Siyagruva Scene, for a short TV programme on the arts in Cape Town.

'Do those look clean to you?' Thabiso demanded, as Disi finished polishing the mirrors in the studio. 'Do them again!'

Disi grinned and sprayed more window cleaner on the sparkling mirrors.

Thabiso wheeled himself across the room and watched closely as Brunette dusted off the pot plants.

'Thabi,' said Brunette, shaking her head, 'take it easy. You're making everyone nervous!'

'I can't, sister,' he said, shaking his head. 'This isn't the time to take it easy!' He wheeled himself off to his office, his mind running over any details he might have missed.

'Hey, Bru,' Rashaad came and slumped on the floor next to Brunette.

'Whassup?'

Rashaad grinned and shook his head.

'I don't know if I'm just imagining this ...'

'Ja?'

'But I can't figure out what's going on with Shelley.'

Brunette bent down low over the plant to dust off the lower leaves. She didn't want Rash to see her face.

'How so?' she asked as innocently as she could.

'Well ... er ... forget it. I don't know how to explain, but she's acting really weird.'

'She's always weird.'

Rashaad shrugged. 'Yeah, I guess so.'

Brunette watched him walk off. She felt really bad about lying to him. What do you do when one friend asks you to keep a secret and the other wants to know the secret?

'Bru!' Shelley pounced on Brunette. 'What did he say?'

'None of your business!'

'You didn't tell him, did you? You promised. You did, didn't you? If you did, I'll never forgive you. That's a promise.'

Brunette sighed, suddenly feeling very tired. I've got to stop getting caught up in other people's business, she thought.

Chapter 5

The phone was ringing again. Brunette cursed under her breath. She was busy plaiting the burgundy extensions into her hair, and this was the third time someone had called. Earlier, Shelley had called to quiz her about what she should say to Rashaad tonight. Brunette had told her that she should tell the truth, but that telling

Rashaad tonight would probably be bad timing. Shelley had not been pleased with that and had slammed the phone down.

Then Sam had called to ask Brunette if she could borrow her boots. She couldn't wear the sandals she had bought because it was raining. Brunette had to tell her that she needed her boots to go with the outfit she was wearing, so Sam had hung up in a huff.

This time it was Thabiso on the phone. Brunette sighed with relief. Thabiso, however, was also really upset.

'Brunette! What am I going to do?'

'About what?'

'Tonight! Tonight! I'm so ...'

'Thabi, everything's perfect. You don't have to worry.'

'Everything ... except me.'

'What d'you mean?'

There was a long silence. Brunette heard Thabiso sigh.

'What's wrong, Thabi?' she urged.

'Nothing. See you later,' Thabiso said quickly and put the phone down.

Brunette went back to doing her hair. Her dad had said the minibus from the TV production company would be picking them up at about six. The show started at eight, but the crew needed time to prepare their lights and cameras. It was already after five, and she hadn't even had a bath.

It was raining lightly by the time the TV minibus drove up to the Artscape Theatre. Brunette was feeling good, sitting up front next to her dad, listening to the jokes being told by the TV crew. As soon as they got to the theatre, the jokes stopped and it was work, work, work, as they unloaded the car. Brunette said 'bye to them and jumped over the puddles. She hurried up the stairs and went into the theatre foyer. Inside, people were already hurrying about, looking very important.

All over the foyer, there were giant posters of Nandi X. The posters read:

'For one night only, internationally acclaimed, locally-made star ...'

In smaller print, one of the overseas reviews raved:

'A class act ... In a league of her own ... African Queen takes contemp dance to dazzling new heights.'

Brunette felt a shiver of excitement run down her spine, but she wished she could find at least one other Siyagruver to hang out with.

She was relieved to see Thabiso wheeling past, looking like a king in a midnight blue jacket, which sat well on his powerful shoulders.

'Hi Thabi!' she called. He stopped and stared. 'Wow! Look at you, my African Queen!'

Brunette nearly kissed him. He always managed to make people feel good.

'Come, let's go over the plans, last minute,' he said.

'Thabs!' sighed Brunette. 'You know everything's going to be just fine.'

'Let's have a drink then,' Thabiso said, still nervous.

They found a free table and Brunette sat down. Thabiso cleared his throat.

'I talked to Nandi X on the phone,' he said shyly.

'Wow, guy! What was she like?'

'She was great, really great. Talked about a lot of things.'

Brunette jumped as Shelley came tottering up behind them, on the highest heels ever, and grabbed Brunette round the neck.

'Percy!'

'Call me Shelley and I'll stop! How do I look?'

Shelley curtsied low in her orange dress.

'Ama-ZING!' Thabiso said.

'And look, all that glitters ...' Sam came shimmying up to the growing crowd in her beaded gold number. She looked stunning too.

'You looking pretty fly, Ms Bru,' she said,

looking Brunette up and down. The three girls posed together and Thabiso shook his head in admiration.

'We should change the name of our group to 'ama-ZING ZING!'

Sam, Brunette and Shelley all kissed him at the same time. He pretended to fight them off, but he was pleased.

'Ladies, please,' he said, smoothing his jacket. 'I need to start making my way to the wheelchair entrance,' he said.

'Wait,' said Shelley. 'Here come Zadie, Disi and Regan.'

Shelley looked behind them to see if there was any sign of Rashaad, but he hadn't arrived yet.

As it was still early, they were the first people in the theatre. Their seats were in the front row.

'Wow, Thabi,' Brunette said, 'right in the front row!'

'I insisted, because of the wheelchair,' said Thabiso. 'And I couldn't very well sit here alone without my peeps.'

'Good plan.'

The theatre was warm and fresh. There was soft music playing. The red curtains held a mystery behind them. Rashaad arrived. He came in from the top and saw his friends sitting at the front.

'Hey!' he called.

They all turned to look at him. Shelley nearly fainted. He looked sooo handsome in a stark white Indian-style suit. His dark skin and black hair made for a striking contrast. He walked down the carpeted stairs with such grace, it was as if he was floating towards her ... and then he was speaking – to her!

'Er ... hum, Percy. Are you all right?'

Horrors of horrors! Everyone was staring at her. She went bright red and nodded quickly. Luckily Raymondo arrived, so that Rashaad's attention was elsewhere for a moment. But then he went to sit next to Raymondo. Shelley felt really stupid. If only she had been a little cooler, he might have been sitting next to her at that very minute.

The theatre was beginning to fill up, and talk and laughter surrounded them. People buzzed around trying to find their seats, crossed the auditorium to say 'Hello' to each other, or sat quietly reading the pro-gramme. But when the lights dimmed, a magical silence fell, and all eyes were focused on the stage as the heavy red curtains at last glided open.

Nandi X lay curled up on the floor. Red lights illuminated her and cast a black shadow on the back wall of the stage, like a cocoon. She was perfectly still. Then the music filled the theatre and Nandi X moved like magic.

Sometimes, she moved so quickly it seemed she was in two places at the same time. At other times, although perfectly still, her whole body was alive with movement. She was a perfect blend of femininity and electric energy as her sheer red dress floated around her. The long red ribbons she carried flicked in time to her sharp hand movements. Everyone was on the edge of their seats.

For an hour she danced, changing from one dazzling outfit to another. Sometimes she danced alone, sometimes with a partner, and sometimes with a troupe; but each time, her grace and elegance enthralled the audience, and, at the end of the performance, there was a storm of applause. Nandi X took five curtain calls. She bowed and smiled and accepted a bouquet of proteas from a little girl.

At last, the curtain closed and the house lights came up. The show was over. Thabiso turned to the Siyagruva team.

'Come, it's time for us to meet that amazing woman!'

In one section of the foyer, waitrons in smart uniforms stood ready to offer the guests the refreshments set out for Nandi X's reception.

The Siyagruva crew huddled together, except for Sam who strode confidently up to the drinks counter. She tried to order a glass of wine, but the waitron asked to see her ID. Sam wasn't very pleased. She ordered a bitter lemon instead.

'Well,' said Thabiso, trying to comfort her, 'you'll be glad you stuck to soft drinks when you have to be up-and-out by nine tomorrow.'

Sam scowled and sucked at the straw in her drink.

Shelley shyly offered Rashaad a drink. He smiled and accepted.

There was a ripple of excitement. Photographers and the TV crew rushed to a particular entrance. Nandi X was coming! The other dancers came out first, smiling and shaking hands, and sometimes signing autographs, as they moved through the crowd. Then Nandi X appeared.

She was much smaller than she looked on stage. She was dwarfed by all the people trying to talk to her. Her manager pushed his way forward and made appointments for interviews. Nandi X answered a few questions, then put her hand up.

'Guys, I really need to relax for just a few minutes,' she said in a flirty tone of voice.

The people crowding her moved back. A waitron was standing by to present her with a drink. Sam noted with pride that Nandi X was also drinking a bitter lemon. Thabiso watched carefully to see when he could approach her. He saw her manager, Dirk, and went up to him instead. Dirk was pleased to meet Thabiso and immediately wheeled him over to Nandi, who was facing the other way. He tapped her lightly on the shoulder.

'Nandi, meet Thabiso, from the Siyagruva Scene,' Dirk said.

Nandi turned and found herself looking straight at Dirk. She followed Dirk's eyes, down to Thabiso, sitting in his wheelchair.

'You're Thabiso?' she asked, confused.

Thabiso nodded and smiled warmly, but Nandi didn't smile back.

'You told me ... you were a dancer!'

'Used to be,' said Thabiso quietly. 'I used to play soccer, too.'

'You didn't say you were ...'

'Disabled?'

'Yes, that. When we talked about including the disabled ... I thought ... you meant the children ...' She was obviously very uncomfortable.

'I had an accident, but I still do what I can. That's what Siyagruva is about for me,' Thabiso said.

She closed her eyes for an instant. Then she bent and shook his hand quickly. But her eyes were already elsewhere. Dirk took over, brisk and business-like.

'Thanks for making all the arrangements. So we're supposed to meet you at Siyagruva Scene at nine tomorrow?'

Thabiso nodded.

He felt drained and was thinking about calling it a night when Brunette came rushing up to him with the TV crew.

'We need to pick up some shots of you meeting Nandi here,' she said excitedly.

Thabiso groaned.

For the camera, Thabiso and Nandi had to pretend to be meeting and talking for the first time. Thabiso noted with interest that Nandi was a natural actress. She went from cold to warm-and-friendly as soon as she heard the words, 'Roll camera!'

At the end of the shoot, she tapped Thabiso's wheelchair and said, 'Thanks, see you tomorrow.' She rushed off so quickly that she almost tripped herself up.

'She's so cool,' sighed Rashaad. Shelley looked at him in panic to see if he meant he liked Nandi like 'that'. It was hard to tell.

'How about going for a drink some-where?' Sam suggested.

Everyone was for the idea except Thabiso, who begged off, saying he was exhausted. He left as soon as he could, asking Mncedisi and Regan to bundle him into a taxi. He didn't want the others to see how disappointed he was about his 'dream' woman.

Chapter 6

It was pretty hard to get up the next day, but once Brunette got going, she was excited about Nandi X's visit to Langa. The others were meeting Nandi at the Siyagruva Scene, but she was going to wait in Langa and take them to the school where Nandi would be giving her workshops with the Siyagruvers.

By the time the minibuses rolled up at about ten, Brunette had organised everything at the school. The children from the community were waiting and were extra-excited to see the TV cameras. They crowded around, jostling one another as they waited for the famous people to get out of the minibuses.

Nandi X was in her element. She was surrounded by children and the cameras were on her. She walked to the hall, which had been cleared for the workshop, children hanging on to both arms. Thabiso wheeled himself slowly over the uneven ground. Brunette came up to him.

'Everything's ready,' she said, proudly.

'Well, I should think so. I expect nothing less,' snapped Thabiso.

Brunette looked at him, a little taken

aback. He was usually so encouraging.

'*Kwentekenjani*? – What's up?' she asked.

Thabiso shook his head. 'You'd better hurry and go and introduce Nandi X to the crowd,' he said, motioning with his head.

'No way. You think I could just take off and leave you like this, without knowing what's up?'

'*Mamela*, Bru. We're supposed to be professionals, so please do as I say.'

Brunette looked at him and she could see that that was the end of the conversation. But she made a note to herself not to let Thabiso go home until she knew what the matter was.

Soon, everyone was caught up in the magic of Nandi X, and the Siyagruvers were also fully involved with the workshop. It was a cold morning but nobody felt it – they were too busy trying out the new steps that Nandi was demonstrating.

The day was a big success. The children really enjoyed the workshop, and Thabiso spent time talking to some of the parents who wanted to know more about where their children could learn dancing. He seemed to be in high spirits again. Nandi was soon whisked away by her manager. Their next appointment would be on Monday afternoon at Westerford High School.

Later, when Brunette looked for Thabiso, she discovered that he had slipped away. She was disappointed, but she couldn't go looking for him because she had invited all the Siyagruvers to her house for something to eat. Auntie Grace had insisted on having some kind of party to show off her catering skills.

Back at the house, Grace was in her element. The house was full to capacity with the TV crew, more of Brunette's dad's friends and the Siyagruvers, but somehow they all found a space to hang out. Grace bustled around in her apron, waving her two-pronged fork like a magic wand.

'Please eat, everyone!' she trilled above the music. 'There's plenty, plenty!'

Brunette was grateful to see the spread Auntie Grace had laid out because everyone had worked up quite an appetite. There was a huge pot of *pap*, mounds of roasted meat, chicken and braaied fish, *chakalaka* gravy, potato salad, green salad, beetroot, baked beans, yellow rice, carrot salad with pineapples and raisins, drinks, and even that

Auntie Grace special: chocolate cake. Every-one tucked in.

Shelley tracked Brunette down and forced her into a corner to ask her what she should do about Rashaad. Brunette groaned.

'I thought you'd decided to tell him last night, already.'

'Well, I didn't really have a chance, did I? We were all stuck together like glue!'

'Percy, really, I think you should just forget it.'

'I don't think he's gay. Did you see the way he looked at Nandi X last night?'

'I look at Nandi X like that and I'm not gay, okay? Everyone admires her,' Brunette sighed. She was getting really fed up with this obsession of Shelley's.

'So, I think I'll go for it.'

'Percy, if it backfires ...'

'Then it backfires.'

'What about the group? It could affect the whole group,' Brunette said cautiously.

'I'll drink a lot and then I'll tell him. If it backfires, I'll just say I was drunk.'

'Mmm ... I can just see Muslim Rashaad falling into your drunken arms ... yeah, that'll really work.'

'Don't be so sarcastic! Really, you're no help at all!'

Shelley marched off and found Sam. Faking boredom, Shelley convinced Sam that they should get some drinks together, go into Brunette's room, and have a real party. Sam was always ready for a party, so they stole away with some bottles of beer, a near-empty box of wine, and the dregs of a whisky bottle.

Shelley drank a bottle of beer, then

slugged back a bit of whisky. She wiped her mouth and handed the bottle to Sam, who tried to drink elegantly. By this time, Shelley had moved on to squeezing the wine from the box, pouring it straight into her mouth. Sam found Brunette's smokes and they lit up and puffed away, suddenly feeling very mellow. Shelley decided to consult Sam.

'Sam, you know how we always joke about Rash's "S-factor"?'

'Well, who else is there to talk about?'

'It's more than that for me. I'm ... in love ... or ... something. I've got to have him.'

Sam sat up, suddenly interested. It was not often that Sam was interested in anything.

'Really?' she sounded excited.

Shelley nodded shyly.

'I'd say go for it!' Sam urged.

'Really? You really think so?'

'Yep, I do.' And Sam went back to the whisky bottle.

Shelley stood up and looked at herself in the mirror. She ran her fingers through her hair and picked up the nearest lipstick on the dressing table. She put it on. It was Brunette's almost black, long-lasting lipstick. The colour didn't work well with her skin, but at that moment she thought she looked pretty good. She ruffled her hair and strutted out of the room.

As luck would have it, there was Rashaad ... going towards the bathroom. She quickly caught up with him. She leaned in very close.

'Hi,' she breathed.

Rashaad laughed nervously. 'Hi, Percy.'

'Where are you going?'

'To wash my hands. Great meal.'

Shelley stood against the bathroom door and Rashaad was very confused. He pointed to the door.

'Can I go in?'

Shelley pressed herself closer to him.

'Oh Rash, don't tell me you don't feel it too?'

'Feel what?'

Shelley put her arms around Rashaad's neck and pulled him towards her. He was staring at her in confusion. He grabbed her arms and swung her around, trying to free himself, but Shelley had different plans. She placed a boozy kiss on his lips. Rash was now pinned against the bathroom door, trapped. He blinked rapidly and then tried to pull away. She held on tighter. Rash caught his breath. His eyes widened.

'Percy,' he said in an urgent whisper.

'Just relax,' she whispered.

'No, Percy ... behind you!'

Shelley turned quickly and saw Brunette's dad disappear through the door to the lounge. She bit her lip.

'Did he ...?'

'Of course, yes,' Rashaad said in a panicky voice. 'I'd better go.'

He swept past her and ran out. Shelley stayed at the bathroom door, swaying slightly.

'Oh no,' she groaned. 'What have I done!'

She stumbled back into Brunette's room. Sam was sitting in front of the mirror, trying on some lipstick. She saw Shelley slump face down on the bed and heard her groan, 'Oh no!'

'What?'

Shelley rolled over. 'I can't believe what I just did!'

'What? What?'

Shelley explained what had happened and made Sam promise not to tell anyone, including Brunette.

'What d'you think? Have I really messed up?' Shelley asked Sam in despair.

'Looks like it, babe,' Sam replied with a nod.

Shelley groaned and flung her face into the pillow. In a muffled voice she cried, 'I'll never be able to face him again.'

'Face who?'

Brunette had just walked in the door. Both Sam and Shelley sat up, staring at her. They had 'guilty' written all over their faces.

'I just saw Rash,' Brunette went on. 'What the hell happened here? And who's been smoking in my room? Really, chicks, this is not cool, really not cool. My dad's seriously angry!'

Shamefaced, Shelley and Sam left Brunette fuming in her room. By this time, she had also seen the lipstick stains on her pillow and she was really mad.

'Like a bunch of kids,' she muttered to herself as she flung the windows open and sprayed some deodorant to cover up the smoky smell. She sniffed. It smelt even worse. Cheap deodorant, stale cigarette smoke and boozy fumes.

'Charming,' she muttered, scowling at herself in the mirror.

Chapter 7

The week seemed endless. Nandi X and her management team had invited the Siyagruvers to a 'thank you' drinks-and-dinner evening. Thabiso was in a foul mood, snapping at everyone. He refused to go to the dinner. Raymondo was in a panic because the dance group were way behind in preparing for the inter-regional competition, which was coming up soon. And both Shelley and Rashaad had been off sick for the past five days.

Brunette's phone had been ringing non-stop. Thabiso had called her to say how disappointed he was about Nandi's shallowness, Shelley had called to try to make Brunette talk to Rashaad, and Rashaad had called in a state of confusion. Eventually, Brunette had allowed Auntie Grace to answer all the calls and make excuses for her – she was doing her homework, washing her hair – whatever.

Then the phone rang again. She heard Grace answer it.

'Brunette, *sana*!' she heard Grace trill. 'It's Nandi X on the phone for you.'

Brunette's heart was thumping as she went to take the call. What could Nandi X want from her?

'This is Brunette,' she said hesitantly into the phone.

'Hi, Brunette.' Nandi sighed.

There was a silence.

'What can I do for you?' Brunette wanted to know.

'I'm calling from a cellphone,' said Nandi. 'I'm in Langa. Can I meet you?'

Brunette gave her the address.

'I'll be there in five,' said Nandi quickly and the phone went dead.

Five minutes later, Nandi climbed out of her rented car, walked across the small garden and knocked on the door. Brunette opened the door straight away. Nandi stood outside, looking thoughtful. She was dressed in black from top to toe, and the silver bangles on her wrist jangled as she reached out her hand to shake Brunette's.

'Thanks for letting me come at such short notice,' she said shyly.

Brunette was taken aback. Imagine that! Nandi X thanking her!

She was leading the way to the lounge, when Auntie Grace swooped on Nandi.

'Hello! Oh, you do us so proud, putting South Africa on the dance map the way you do. And now, here you are and it's really ...'

Nandi X forced a smile.

'I'm sorry, Auntie Grace,' Brunette said quickly. 'Nandi has some urgent business and we need to talk privately.'

Grace was offended and she stiffly offered Nandi some tea, but Nandi declined. Grace went out with a hurt expression on her face. Brunette felt bad. It was too much. It seemed that someone was always getting hurt in one way or another.

Brunette looked at Nandi, the question in her eyes – What's up?

'Oh, Brunette,' sighed Nandi, 'I had to talk to someone from Siyagruva.'

'About?'

'I think you know ... Thabiso.'

'What about him?'

'Well, you know he's refused to come to the farewell dinner. It's bad for publicity. I know that he thinks I'm just some stuck-up prima donna.'

Brunette bit her lip. Should she say what she was thinking? She took a deep breath and began.

'Well, you act really strangely when you're around him, you know. Thabiso was a great dancer. He doesn't like being disabled, but he does the best he can to look on the bright side of life. He really admires you and yet you treated him really badly. I don't think he deserves to be treated like that.'

Nandi stood up suddenly. She looked a bit put out, but she nodded in agreement.

'I know,' she said quietly.

'And,' Brunette continued, 'I think you should be having this conversation with him, not me.'

'So, I guess you think I'm stuck-up too?'

'No, not at all! I think you're a fantastic dancer, but you could learn something from Thabi about ...'

'I have a terrible fear,' Nandi blurted out in a half whisper, 'I have a fear about becoming disabled. It's funny. I can deal with kids who were born that way, but I can't bear to look at him. He used to dance and now he can't even walk! Nothing in the world makes that okay. It's an awful, awful thing to happen to someone!'

'It's his life now,' Brunette said quietly. 'I think you should make an effort to see him and explain. You owe him that.' She was feeling quite brave now.

Nandi nodded reluctantly and took down Thabiso's address. She stood up to leave and Brunette opened the door for her. Nandi suddenly hugged Brunette really hard.

'Your dance group is doing great things,' she said. 'Keep it up.'

She went to the kitchen and apologised to Grace.

'You have a great daughter,' she said to her. Grace didn't try to correct her mistake, but, instead, gave Brunette a great big smile. Brunette smiled back. For the first time, she felt that she really meant it.

Brunette was relieved that the thing

between Nandi X and Thabiso was out in the open. So, she decided to get Shelley and Rashaad to talk about their problem too. She called them both and told them she wanted to see them. She refused to take any feeble excuses. They arranged to meet at Siyagruva before the farewell dinner.

Shelley and Rashaad were really shy, and Brunette had to push them to talk about their feelings. Shelley apologised to Rashaad for giving him a drunken kiss, without his permission. Rash shyly admitted that it was the first kiss he'd ever had.

'It was quite nice, boozy or not,' he said jokingly. 'But a little more talking beforehand might have saved us both a lot of confusion!'

'I was only thinking about myself,'

Shelley admitted. 'It won't happen again. I should know better – I should know that ... er ... it takes two to tango.'

'I'll dance to that!' said Rashaad, jumping up, sweeping across the studio to put some music on. He bowed to Shelley and they launched themselves across the room in an exaggerated tango.

Other Siyagruva members arrived and joined them in their crazy dance. Everyone needed to release the tension that had been building up. Then Nandi arrived. She watched, laughing and clapping, and then joined in, dancing with Raymondo.

Everyone was so busy dancing they didn't see Thabiso slip into the room to watch the dancers stalking and dipping across the floor. In the mirror, Nandi saw Thabiso. She bowed her way out of her dance with

Raymondo, and walked across to him.

Brunette held her breath as she saw Thabiso and Nandi touch hands tenderly. They didn't say anything to each other, but it was obvious that they had talked and come to some understanding.

Thabiso clapped his hands and called, 'Everyone, gather round!'

The music was switched off and everyone stood around waiting expectantly.

'Nandi has a few words to say, then, no more speeches – just party, party, party!'

Everyone clapped, happy to see Thabiso back to his old self.

'My dear Siyagruvers,' Nandi began, 'I travel all over the world and meet a lot of people. I know that there's something special in everyone, and people believe that there's something special about me. But, when I met Thabiso here, I was confronted by my deepest fear. I thought, what would happen to me if I couldn't ever dance again? Who would I be? I love dancing and it's my life, but here with you, I remembered something really important that I had forgotten. About the value of friendship and truth, and the courage to be able to go on, no matter what. Thank you, Siyagruvers. Thank you!'

Nandi had tears in her eyes. Thabiso patted her hand and she smiled.

'Thank you,' he said simply. He turned to the others. 'Now, let's go and eat!'

Everyone cheered.

They filed out, but Thabiso hung back, turning off the lights. Brunette caught up with him in the office. In the dark, they listened to the laughter and chatter of the others from beyond the door. Then Thabiso spoke.

'She told me what you said, Bru. Thank you.'

Brunette sighed. 'You, Thabs, you never talk about the bad days.'

'I have bad days, I do. But my worst fear has already happened. Poor Nandi, she's still going to have to find out who she is when the lights go off. Look at it this way, Bru. I'm a lot freer than most. I was forced to think about life and I decided to do all the things that make me happy. I'm doing what I love with people I like – and that's as good as it gets, hey?'

'I'll say,' said Brunette, nodding. 'I've decided to make some changes too.'

'Oh yeah?'

'Mmm ... giving up some stuff that's not so cool.'

'Like chocolate?' Thabiso's voice was teasing in the dark.

'Give up chocolate? Never! But trying to fix people's loves and lives ... definitely!'

Thabiso squeezed Brunette's hand.

'Then I've been one of the lucky ones,' he said quietly. 'Now let's go and eat!'

SIYAGRUVA

A series of novels for South African teens

IN THE FAST LANE

NOKUTHULA MAZIBUKO

Remember, there are people affected by HIV as well as people infected by HIV. This is something Brunette and Samantha have no reason to worry about, until they go on holiday to the home of Brunette's mother in Soweto. Suddenly they're living with HIV and have to learn – quick!

'We can't deny these things, they happen, and we have to know how to cope.'
A reader

S I Y A G R U V A

A series of novels for South African teens

DIVINE DUMP DANCER

RUSSELL H KASCHULA

From the dumps to divining, from despair to dancing! This happens to Mncedisi when he and his mother come to the city. Some people are called to fulfil their role and responsibility to family and community. Could you travel the journey Mncedisi has to?

'He's not a quitter, he has courage and strength – and he's a great dancer!'
A reader

SIYAGRUVA

A series of novels for South African teens

HIGH HEELS AND HIJACK

NIBOR NALAM

Of course, Shelley knows better than her mother! Or does she? Tonight is a big night for her – but it could end in disaster. Nothing gets Thabiso down! But what happens the night he's not in his wheel-chair? Can his wits pull him through?

'Young people deal with hate, jealousy, friendship and danger every day – and comedy!'
A reader